Learning How to Ask Someone for Help

Susan Kent

The Rosen Publishing Group's
PowerKids Press™
New York

For Wendy Schwartz, who is great at giving help.

Published in 2001 by The Rosen Publishing Group, Inc.
29 East 21st Street, New York, NY 10010

First Edition

Book Design: Maria E. Melendez

Photo Credits: Cover and Title Page, pp. 8, 12, 15, 16, 19, 20 by Debra Rothstein-Brewer; pp. 4 © Corbis-Bettman; pp. 7, 11 © Index Stock Photography.

Kent, Susan, 1942–
    Learning how to ask someone for help / by Susan Kent.
        p. cm.—(The violence prevention library)
    Includes index.
    Summary: Describes problems that children may face, and how they should ask for help in solving them.
    ISBN 0-8239-5612-1 (lib. bdg. : alk. paper)
    1. Problem solving in children—Juvenile literature. [1. Problem solving.] I. Title. II. Series.
BF723.P8.K46 2000
155.4'1343—dc21   99-044836

Manufactured in the United States of America

Contents

Everyone Has Problems

We all have problems every day. Some problems are big. Some are small. Some problems we can solve by ourselves. When Zach's dog, Belle, ran away, he searched the neighborhood until he finally found her. He felt good about finding his dog and getting her home safely by himself.

For some problems we need help from others. When Mary fell out of a treehouse and broke her leg, she needed help. Mary's doctors, nurses, parents, teachers, and her friends all helped her. She could not have fixed the problem by herself.

Zach was very upset when his dog ran away. He knew he had a big problem to solve, and he did, on his own.

Speaking Up

Sometimes you have to speak up to get the help you need. When you **communicate** your feelings, problems, or questions to others, they can get you help. If you do not communicate, people may not know that something is bothering you. It can be hard for others to know that you have a problem if you do not tell them.

If you want to talk to someone, like your older sister, and she is busy, try to plan a special time to speak with her. Finding the right time to talk to others is an important part of asking for help.

This little girl asked her older sister to help her read her favorite book.

Asking for Help Can Be Hard

Sometimes it is not so easy to ask for help. It can be hard to **admit** that you need help. You might be afraid that the person you ask will not want to help. You might not know the right person to ask, or what kind of help you need.

Even if it is hard to ask, dealing with problems by yourself can be even harder. It is important to remember that people often like to help, but they need to be asked. It is also important to keep trying to find help even if the first person you ask cannot give you the help you need.

This young boy asks his mom for help with a problem. She is busy, but she takes time to listen and help her son.

9

Asking Friends for Help

Friends are usually glad to help. When Althea wanted to put on a play in her backyard, she asked Sara and Tim to help her. They all had great ideas and made the play extra special! When Sara did not do well on her math test, Tim agreed to help her study. Sara did much better on her next math test. She thanked Tim for his help.

Do not be shy about asking friends for help. Some day a friend might need to ask you for help. Helping each other is part of what being good friends is all about.

It's a good idea to ask your friends for help. Working together helps solve problems. ▶

Power from the people,
protected and guaranteed
by the Constitution
of the United States of America,
has kept a union of states,
now grown to fifty,
together for more than two hundred years.

Needing Help at School

You might need help at school for many different kinds of problems, and that is okay. When you have tried your best, but still have trouble learning, ask a **tutor** to work with you. When you have problems at home or with your classmates, you can talk to your **guidance counselor**. You may not always know who to ask for help. It is okay to ask different people. You might ask someone who can't help you, but this person might know someone who can help you. Don't give up until you find just the right person to help you with your problem.

When you don't understand a lesson, ask your teacher to explain it again.

Asking for Help at School

It might make you feel **frustrated** or **embarrassed** that you need extra help at school. You might also feel angry that you need help when others don't. Try not to let it get you down. Instead of feeling sad or mad, remember that you are good at many things. You may be great at sports, music, or art. Keep enjoying these things, but get help for the subjects that give you trouble.

If you get the help you need, you will soon feel better about those harder subjects, too, and you'll feel great about yourself!

When you get help with the subjects or activities you find difficult, you can improve and get better at them. ▶

Hernando Asks for Help

A gang of boys at school teases Hernando because he speaks with an accent. He asks for help. His parents say, "Ignore them." His older sister suggests making a joke, but nothing seems to work.

Finally Hernando asks his teacher for help. She gives a lesson to the class on **immigration**. She asks some students, including Hernando, to tell the class about the countries they came from. When the boys understand what Hernando's family went through to get to America, they don't tease him anymore.

Hernando talks to the class about the country he came from. He is glad he asked his teacher for help.

Deena Asks for Help

Deena sees Benjy selling drugs at school. She tries to talk to him, but he tells her to mind her own business. She does not want to get Benjy in trouble, but she knows drugs will get both Benjy and the kids who buy them into even bigger trouble.

She thinks about who to ask for help. Finally she tells the guidance counselor, who helped her when her parents got divorced. Deena trusts her. The guidance counselor talks to Benjy and helps him deal with his problem. Deena is happy she thought of a good person to ask.

Deena talks to her guidance counselor about a serious problem. Deena feels better knowing her guidance counselor will help. ▸

Help From Your Community

There are many people in your community who are there to help. You can ask a police officer to help you if you are lost or hurt. You can ask a doctor to help you when you are sick. You can see a **therapist** if you are feeling sad or confused about something. You can go to your religious leader for help with questions about life.

Be sure to ask for the special help you want or need. Remember when you have a problem, you are not alone. You are part of a family, a school community, and a neighborhood.

There are lots of people whom you can ask for help. This boy asks a police officer for help.

Keep Asking

You might not get help right away. If your father is busy, you may have to wait for help on your homework. Your mother might not have heard you when you asked her for help, so you need to ask again. If you don't get the help you need, it is okay to ask again. If the person you asked can't help you, ask someone else. Keep asking until you get the help you need. You deserve it!

One day, someone might ask you for help. You can help them the same way people have helped you. We all need help, and we all need to help each other.

Glossary

admit (ad-MIT) To say something is real or true.

communicate (kuh-MYOO-nih-kayt) To give or exchange information or news.

embarrassed (im-BAYR-ist) Feeling uncomfortable or ashamed.

frustrated (FRUS-tray-tid) When you feel angry or sad because you cannot do anything about a certain situation.

guidance counselor (GY-dins KOWN-suh-ler) Someone who helps students solve personal problems, problems with schoolwork, or problems with other people.

immigration (IH-muh-gray-shun) The act of coming to a new country to live there.

therapist (THER-uh-pist) A person who is trained to work with people to help them understand their feelings.

tutor (TOO-ter) Someone who teaches one student or a small group of students.

Index